Table of Contents

I0015364

What is Proximity and IoT?

Every year, we're seeing all new kinds of technology emerge. More importantly, these technologies are changing the way we interact with the world and with each other. The now famous "Internet of Things" represents a huge shift in how we imagine technology and its role in the world. This is important not just on the individual-level but for businesses, visitors, employees, and everything in between.

Then, there's proximity. The IoT is tearing down a wall when it comes to communications. Proximity technology is about making interactions more practical. It's about using data that is physically relevant and timely. In short, it's the missing piece of the physical-to-digital puzzle.

What is the Internet of Things (IoT)?

The Internet of Things (or IoT for short) is a term for a variety of technologies that describe a number of different ways to connect physical things to the internet. As a result, any item can become smart and context-aware, providing highly personalized experiences and gathering rich data about what's happening in the real world.

In reality, the IoT is a pretty simple concept. All kinds of items or "things" are wirelessly connected. For consumers, this can mean a lot of exciting results: smart homes, smart offices, smart *entire lives.* Your wearable talks to your spoon talks to your daily planner. Everything is automated. And that's where the term Internet of Everything comes from.

Why is the IoT really important?

Beyond the shiny consumer sphere, the IoT is leading to very meaningful changes and serious shifts in how we view the world. It's not just about the rise of AI and machine learning. It's about bridging the physical and the digital. Your movements in the real world will have a digital result, and your digital actions will create physical changes. Yes, the IoT is about your wearables, but it's also about building a completely new kind of ecosystem.

One key component here is the power of proximity. Whether it's push notifications, indoor navigation, or anything else powered by a smart device, proximity information enables a new world of opportunities. This leads us to our next question...

What is Proximity?

Some call it proximity marketing, but, in fact, its opportunities extend far beyond the reach of just marketing.

Proximity means that an IoT-enabled object reacts and changes according to your location. Let's look at a smart home for example. You can "teach" your home to adjust the lighting based on your preferences and time, but wouldn't it be better if the lights switched on as you walk into your apartment or change automatically as you go from room to room?

By adding another layer of contextual information to IoT-enabled objects, it gets them to serve you and your needs at the right place at the right time. This technology already exists, so it's up to businesses and consumers to find the most important use cases.

So what is Proximity Marketing?

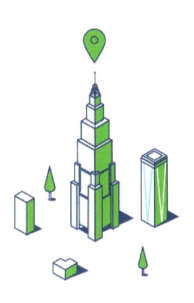

Proximity marketing is by no means new. Local and in-store advertising have been snagging customers at the moment where it matters most for decades. Vague advertisements you see on a television or a pop-up ad could be appealing, but they are rarely tailored to you and your present situation. They are less actionable and require you to get up and actually visit the store or other location.

Proximity is about reaching a user or customer based on their actual physical relationship to other objects. For example, are they on a bus? Are they approaching a particular coffee shop? Are they exiting your store? Technology means businesses can choose when to send which messages and to whom in order to achieve the best results and satisfy customers.

How technology makes proximity happen

There are several ways to bring proximity to a solution. Geofencing, NFC, and QR codes have been adding proximity to solutions for years. The moment you enter a space, your phone buzzes with a message. These methods, however, aren't always practical. NFC and QR are passive, meaning users can walk right by an important message. Geofencing isn't capable of targeting a specific location, limiting the kinds of messages that can be sent. But Bluetooth is now stepping up to the plate.

The role of beacons

Bluetooth beacons play a hugely important role in both the future of the IoT and proximity. Beacons have been of growing importance in proximity for a number of reasons including:

- High penetration rates: over 90%[1] of smartphones are equipped with Bluetooth
- Long range: Bluetooth can broadcast up to 100m
- Energy efficiency: BLE is far more energy efficient than many other methods

All of these factors also make Bluetooth the prime candidate for standard of the IoT revolution. As items become smarter, they'll *all* need to speak the same language. Bluetooth can connect all the moving parts and 'things' to create a consumer-friendly network and power the automation required to create fully seamless, wireless ecosystem.

Proximity and relevance

On top of just being cool, proximity offers serious dividends to companies who invest in it wisely. Proximity means knowing where your customers and assets are and interacting with them in ways that are meaningful. Without proximity technology, marketing efforts can fall flat by not addressing the customer at the right moment in their journey.

For example, you design a campaign that offers real, valuable savings on your customers' favorite products. You understand your audience and craft great visuals and copy. You're set to launch with a bang. Then your customer comes on the

1
https://www.bluetooth.com/news/pressreleases/2014/04/08/spike-in-bluetoothtechnology-penetration-in-hub-devices-leads-to-increased-bluetooth-smart-adoption-

premises. They receive a welcome message via text. The same text that everyone else receives. A general "hey, thanks for coming by! Here's 10% off when you spend >$100."

Customers move through the store and through the in-store advertising that repeats the same deal. It's a great deal. But what makes it different? What makes it really actionable?

With Bluetooth, that same business could send out more timely and targeted messages. If the customer approaches the cafe, they may receive 10% off a coffee. If the customer has been viewing seasonal products online, they could be notified about promotions relevant to their expressed interests. This is the difference between vague promotions and smart proximity marketing. Beacons offer businesses the chance to use their creativity and power campaigns that benefit both parties.

What are the different types of Proximity Marketing?

There are several methods for adding proximity to a business or marketing campaign. If you've ever gone to use free WiFi and were met with a local ad, you've seen it first hand.

Common types of proximity marketing:

- WiFi
- NFC
- Geofencing
- BLE
- QR

What is a beacon?

So, what IS a beacon? Beacons are awesome little high-tech tools, and we're excited to tell you all about them! Consider this your formal introduction to BLE beacon technology. Enjoy!

A beacon is a small Bluetooth radio transmitter.

It's kind of like a lighthouse: it repeatedly transmits a single signal that other devices can see. Instead of emitting visible light, though, it broadcasts a radio signal that is made up of a combination of letters and numbers transmitted on a regular interval of approximately 1/10th of a second. A Bluetooth-equipped device like a smartphone can "see" a beacon once it's in range, much like sailors looking for a lighthouse to know where they are.

But what is a beacon like on the inside?

What do they look like? Beacons are very small, simple devices. If you crack one open, you won't find thirty motherboards and oodles of wires. You'll find a CPU, radio, and batteries. Beacons often use small lithium chip batteries (smaller and more powerful than AA batteries) or run via connected power like USB plugs. They come in different shapes and colors, may include accelerometers, temperature sensors, or unique add-ons but all of them have one thing in common—they transmit a signal.

What is a beacon actually transmitting?

It's not throwing just any old message into the air. It's transmitting a unique ID number that tells a listening device which beacon it's next to.

Really, it's just a code name.

How can I interact with beacons?

For example, when a shopping mall installs beacons in their shop, all of the beacons will have certain IDs, registered in their dedicated app. This means a smartphone app can immediately recognize that the incoming ID is important and that it's from that particular mall. The ID, however, has little meaning on its own; it's entirely up to an app or other program to recognize what it means.

What happens next? That depends on what the owner has programmed it to do. One code could trigger the app to send a coupon. Another could offer navigation services. The possibilities are nearly endless. All the beacon has to do is connect your exact location to the app, and the rest is up to the program.

What's happening behind the computer screen?

Beacons are incredibly misunderstood. They are not tracking you. They're not interested in that.

They're just broadcasting a signal. Here's why this signal can trigger so many different things.

An online platform, lets you manage, configure, and update all your beacons. From there, you may develop your own app or use a further program called a Content Management System. These programs allow you to associate links, images, videos, and texts with individual beacons. Many of these platforms are made to be highly user-friendly. This means they are often sleek and easy-to-use with no coding required. For example, a program could let a museum owner add brand new capabilities to their gallery app (like quizzes or audio guides) just by typing questions or text. The program then does all the hard work automatically and stores everything in the cloud so your app can easily access it.

How do beacons connect to the web?

You've probably heard of Bluetooth. It's present in 90% of all phones and has been around since the 1990s. So what's changed? Why is it so important now? While many consumers don't use Bluetooth on a daily basis, it's hugely important to the Internet of Things. Being in 90% of the world's phones, Bluetooth technology means beacons are compatible with devices consumers use on a daily basis around the globe.

Bluetooth provides the infrastructure for the entire beacon ecosystem. It's a standard for sending data over short distances, a wireless technology not so dissimilar from WiFi. This is why beacon hardware can be simple. There is already a web of Bluetooth around you that can connect beacons and smart devices and almost anything else.

Why do we say "BLE beacons"?

BLE stands for Bluetooth Low Energy. It's a power-efficient version of Bluetooth originally introduced in 2010. BLE's low energy needs are vital to beacons, as it allows them to run for years on tiny coin-cell batteries. It also consumes far less energy than the old and clunky Bluetooth. In fact, BLE is a major driver in the IoT, allowing technology to last longer with smaller parts.

The next question is, how do beacons actually enable connecting and transferring data?

How does a beacon communicate?

Beacon hardware is relatively simple, but the way it triggers actions can get a little complicated. Every system is a little different, but here's how a beacon communicates, in a nutshell:

The beacon sends out its ID numbers about ten times every second (sometimes more, sometimes less, depending on its settings). A nearby Bluetooth-enabled device, like your phone, picks up that signal. When a dedicated app recognizes it, it links it to an action or piece of content stored in the cloud and displays it to the user. You can "teach" your app how to react to a beacon signal by developing using third-party tools.

Infographic: What are Beacons and What Do They Do?

Couldn't the beacon data just be hardcoded into the app?

Why go through the cloud? It sounds so unnecessary!

The #1 reason you don't want data hardcoded on your phone is space. Keeping content on the cloud makes your app light and keeps your phone from being bogged down. No one wants to download bulky apps-especially when they're on the go.

Reason #2 is that content attached to beacons does change. But, remember how beacons only broadcast an ID? That ID doesn't change too often but the content behind it does. Say you're a store owner and you want to run a new sales campaign or add a promotion to your existing offerings. If your beacon data is hardcoded, you would have to completely re-release the app. Storing data in the cloud means beacons can be updated almost instantly. It means the app doesn't have to be altered or re-coded. Once the information is online, it's ready to go to the beacon. So, what is a beacon going to do to help you? Let's try an example.

So, what is a beacon going to do to help you? Let's try an example.

You're going on a trip to some far-off country—nice! But you don't speak the language—crap!

On the way to the hotel, you arrive at a big train station. The station is huge, and you have no idea where to go. How can you get directions that are reliable, clear, and in a language you understand?

Luckily, the train station owner planned for problems just like this. You see a sign indicating that the train station has an app. You download it. A beacon placed on the wall sends out a continuous signal, and, once you activate the app, you're able to make use out of it. The app takes the beacon ID and checks what information is paired with that particular beacon.

It recognizes that you are standing in front of the donut shop by Gate 14. You enter your destination, and the app generates a clear map to show you the way there. When you turn down the wrong path, it redirects you.

Since you have plenty of time, the app also lets you know that the coffee shop to your left has a special deal going on. The app tells you all the train schedules and delays for the station.

You catch your train on time and realize it's not so stressful after all.

Where did beacon technology begin?

Today's beacons began with the introduction of iBeacon. iBeacon is simply a protocol that lets Bluetooth devices transmit very small bits of data.

Then Google entered the scene. In 2015, Google came out with Eddystone, their iBeacon alternative. Since then, **iBeacon and Eddystone** have ruled the proximity market.

Now, beacon technology is continuing to develop with cooler capabilities, better hardware, and more diverse solutions.

Interval	Tx Power	Expected Range	Expected Battery Life *
100ms	3 (-12 dBm)	35 m (115')	Up to 7 months
300ms (default)	3 (-12 dBm)	35 m (115')	Up to 2 years
1000ms or 1s	3 (-12 dBm)	35 m (115')	Up to 4 years

*Assuming optimal environmental conditions.

What are all these numbers?! (reading beacon specs)

What is a beacon packet? Do you need those? Here are some notes on beacon specs and details.

- Battery life: Most beacons start with an 18-24 month battery life. However, some beacons with certain requirements and uses last some 6-8 months. Beacons with energy-saving capabilities can last over 5 years.
  How can beacons last so long with such tiny batteries? Easy! They don't actually work that hard. They let Bluetooth do all the work, and Bluetooth is incredibly energy efficient.
- Supported format: Does your beacon use the iBeacon protocol? Eddystone? Beacons usually support both of these and sometimes the hardware manufacturer's own format (like AltBeacon).
- Interval: How often can the beacon transmit its message? How often you need your beacon to transmit depends on your specific scenario. (ms=millisecond)
- Tx Power: The Transmission Power describes how far a beacon can transmit data. This can be as little as 4 meters, but many reach some 50-90 meters. However, it is not necessary that this number be humongous. A 50-meter range beacon can be just as useful as a 90-meter depending on the specific use.
- Packets: A beacon's "packet" is the data it transmits. This just describes the kind of information it is able to transmit. For example, iBeacon contains one packet (iBeacon itself) while Eddystone has three separate ones.
- Sensors: Now, beacons are coming out with extra capabilities. They may include accelerometers, light or movement sensors.
- NFC / RFID: Beacons are still very new. For some users, it's highly important that legacy technologies (like NFC and RFID tags) and beacons work together.
- Price: Beacons can cost as little as $5. Will such a cheap beacon be worth it? Well, that really depends on what you want, but many users will find that ultra-cheap beacons simply don't get the job done. Expect one ordinary beacon to run $15-25.

What is a beacon used for?

Retail

Education

Culture

Airports

Events

Office

Hospitality

So beacons are cool and all... but what is a beacon really used for by businesses? Lots of things!

What are common use cases?

Proximity technology is still really popular in retail settings. Pay a visit to Macy's, American Eagle, or the Tokyo airport, and you may find beacons in place. But beacons are becoming even more popular each year. This means you're likely to find them just about anywhere you move.

Beacons are already being used for:

- Tracking: One of the beacons' more practical use cases is something many of us would never have guessed. In manufacturing and transport, managers need to know exactly where goods are at any given time. By attaching beacons, they can always have that information. In fact, they can even see the information from previous days or weeks.
- Navigation: Creating accurate "GPS for indoor navigation" is a popular beacon use case. What Google Maps does for the outdoors, beacons can do for the indoors. They can tell you where you are and where you're going in a museum, festival, or train station.
- Interaction: Beacons can make reactions automated and trigger events. When you enter a room, the projector starts. It sends notifications or acts as a loyalty card. If you make a purchase at your local cafe, beacons help the app register that you were there. On your tenth entry, you get a free latte—awesome!
- Security: Whether it's making sure patients don't go in the wrong wing or alerting factory workers to dangerous changes, beacons can automatically send notifications (either to app users or property owners) about a safety issue. Beacons can also be paired with geofencing to add an extra layer to data security.

- Analysis: Data is one of the biggest tools at a company's disposal. Beacons help generate data on where customers are going or where common problems occur on an assembly line. The online platform can store information on which beacons are being triggered and how users are interacting with them.

In the previous section we discussed what are beacons but then there's iBeacon, Eddystone, and what else? Here we'll explain the difference between iBeacon vs. Eddystone, their histories, and what makes them each uniquely cool.

A beacon is a small device that transmits a Bluetooth signal at regular intervals. This signal is broadcast in a certain format, a communication protocol that describes the string of characters and numbers that make up the signal. The two most common protocols that beacons use are iBeacon and Eddystone! However, despite being incredibly similar (in that they both power beacon technology) the two standards are also fundamentally different. Much like Google and Apple, they fill different spaces in the market and, really, aren't fundamentally interchangeable. They're both being great tools. Here's what you need to know about them.

What is iBeacon?

The history behind the beacon's initiatory protocol

In short: The iBeacon profile is the first, and currently most commonly discussed, communication protocol around. It is not a physical hardware but rather the language used to power the physical "beacon" technology we picture. Developed by Apple, it is natively supported in iOS and has deep integrations with the mobile OS. Although the iBeacon profile works on other mobile operating systems, it works best in the environment for which it was designed: iPhones and iPads.

The full story: iBeacon technology has been around since 2013. Apple first announced the exciting new platform at the 2013 Worldwide Developers Conference, though its release went almost unnoticed in a number of ways. In reality, it would take quite some time for other companies to build up an ecosystem of products and use cases that put the technology to work.

It would also take time for the world to understand the fundamental nature of the protocol. Due perhaps to public assumption that anything from Apple would function out-of-the-box, consumers continue to misunderstand iBeacon. The internet is full of opportunities to "buy iBeacons"—whatever that means. In reality, you'll be buying a piece of hardware (often protocol-agnostic) and then choosing which language (iBeacon or Eddystone) to use.

To prove they're not all talk, Apple activated iBeacons across their 254 stores in the US. This was followed by a number of early adopters with similar retail usages for the technology. Since then, the protocol has been growing in popularity and, more importantly, growing through different verticals.

How does iBeacon work?

In short: A beacon using an iBeacon profile contains a combination of letters and numbers, broken up into specific groups. Each code is unique for every beacon, and a mobile application will only take action when it recognizes the data related to that beacon. Once a beacon is detected by an application, some kind of action is triggered: a push alert to the home screen, a prompt to log something into the phone, connect to a server, and so on.

This is the iBeacon's first major distinction from Eddystone: it has the ability to wake up apps on both iOS and Android. For some businesses, this is a huge deal. Users don't have to actively have a program running. They don't have to enter any numbers or scan anything. They need only have the overarching app installed. For stores in a mall, this could be one app for the mall or a larger app used by several stores around the globe. This is the catch: your users absolutely must have the right app installed. However, once they do, you can send and collect far more data. When users think about beacon technology, they picture iBeacon and the ability to completely automate the interaction from physical movement to receiving a personalized, location- and profile-based notification.

However, this exchange is much less magical and mysterious than it sounds. The beacon is simply broadcasting an ID number that is then used the related app and program to return results. It's up to developers to make use of the simple beacon data.

More importantly, these numbers are simply assigned to a physical location. While the numbers stay the same, the location with which they're associated may be changed when necessary. Their importance lies in the database connecting identifier numbers with a physical location. This is true for both iBeacon and Eddystone.

iBeacon's signal contains three main pieces of information.

- Unique Universal Identifier (UUID): the beacon's most general information. For example, this beacon belongs to this person.
- Major: the beacon's most general spatial information. For example, this beacon is located in store #8.
- Minor: a more minute piece of information. For example, this is the beacon in aisle.

iBeacon technology for developers and techies

Best practices and more detailed information can be found on Apple's own write-up about iBeacon. This is actually a very interesting, not so complicated, read, so if you're just curious to read more about the technicalities, you can find it.[2]

What is Eddystone?

The history behind the open protocol

The Eddystone format is a new and open communication protocol developed by Google with Android users in mind.

We often compare beacons to a lighthouse; they're just simple objects constantly sending out a signal. Perhaps that's the reason Google named their beacon format after the Eddystone Lighthouse in the UK. More importantly, though strikingly similar to iBeacon, it is distinctly Google (or, at least, non-Apple). The protocol is now known for being "open," created with the input and collaboration of several companies. Instead of being created to power highly specific user-facing apps, its key qualities are interoperability and long-term strength.

This is made clear in its relation and importance to the Physical Web. The Physical Web is more like the overarching idea we have about wireless connectivity. It's a form the IoT could take—making the digital and physical work together through beacons.

In the end, though the two formats are often mixed up, they represent pretty different ways of using the IoT.

---

[2] https://developer.apple.com/ibeacon/Getting-Started-with-iBeacon.pdf

How does Eddystone work?

Much of how Eddystone works is the same as iBeacon. But there's extended functionality beyond that. Eddystone exists as four different frames: Eddystone-UID, Eddystone-URL, Eddystone-TLM, and Eddystone-EID. The UID works more or less exactly as iBeacon does: it broadcasts a short code at a regular interval. Eddystone-URL broadcasts a URL that can be viewed by anyone with a Bluetooth-enabled smartphone whether they have your app installed or not, and Eddystone-TLM broadcasts some telemetry data about any attached sensors and the status of the beacon itself. This could easily be used to power data collection or triggers. In short, an Eddystone beacon does nearly everything iBeacon does with some added features.

Any beacon can broadcast both Eddystone and iBeacon formats interchangeably using our packet interleaving feature.

Eddystone sends 4 packets:

- Unique ID (UID) is a unique static ID (similar to the UUID, Majors, and Minors) with two parts: Namespace and Instance.
- URL includes a compressed URL that can be directly used by the end-user (think Physical Web!).
- TLM is another packet not found in iBeacon. It contains telemetry data that's great for fleet management purposes.
- EID is an added security measure.
  Read more on packets and IDs here.

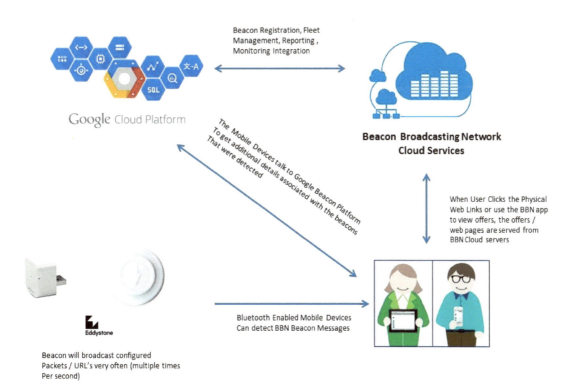

Eddystone for developers and techies

Due to the open nature of the protocol, Eddystone can be used in a number of different ways. This write-up[3] from Google is a bit more complicated than that from Apple, so casual perusers beware.

Real-word example unique to Eddystone and the Physical Web

One of our favorite examples combines beacons with public transit with the tech-loving city of London. Proxama is one of the first location service providers certified by Google engineers. They worked with Exterion Media, a major and international media company to deploy the world's first consumer-focused Physical Web campaign in London using beacons. Though this isn't the first time Proxama used the Physical Web and Eddystone, it's one of the first times the world has seen the technology in action in such a big and complex way.

Their MyStop program catered to passengers on London buses, sending information about transit times and updates including how close they were their selected stop. Instead of forgetting their stop or getting lost, that meant users could simply enter their destination and wait for notification. On top of offering cool and useful information, this had the added benefit of being done through Eddystone instead of iBeacon—meaning branded and unwanted content can easily be silenced or ignored altogether.

Which one, which one?

The differences between the two are minor enough that end-users will likely not know the difference unless you're implementing a Physical Web-based campaign. However, the coding and capabilities are a bit different as are their speculative outlook for the future. Apple is great at doing Apple: iBeacon is great at being relatively simple to implement. It's also a proprietary software totally owned and controlled by Apple. Eddystone is going the other direction. They're open to developers and published openly on GitHub. But it may not be so easy to implement. Eddystone also has those extra packets used for fleet management and security.

The final decision may come down to developers and what they want to work with, but this gives us a better understanding of what sets the two apart. Plus, with packet interleaving, you don't have to choose between iBeacon and Eddystone.

---

[3] https://developers.google.com/beacons/overview

Moreover, there are more formats on their way. Though none have yet to pick up traction, it's likely those looking for more specialized options will find more formats available in the future.

Industry Trends (2016 Review)

Beacon Technology Market size was estimated at over USD 170 million in 2016 with a CAGR of over 80% from 2017 to 2024.

Beacon Technology Market Share, By Application, 2016

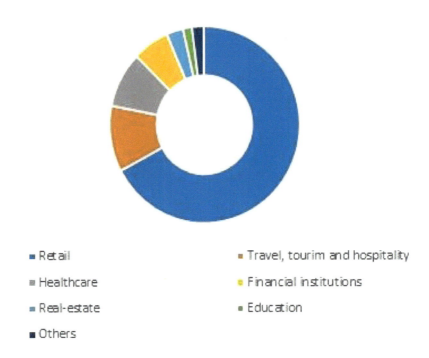

- ■ Retail
- ■ Healthcare
- ■ Real-estate
- ■ Others
- ■ Travel, tourim and hospitality
- ■ Financial institutions
- ■ Education

The beacon technology market is gaining momentum due to consistently growing demand for proximity-based marketing solutions in the retail environment. As there is an increasing need for personalized service experience by customers, retailers are exploring modern technological alternatives for improving in-store advertising efforts. With smartphones poised to emerge as the ubiquitous technology of the 21st century, their rapid adoption around the world is boosting the growth of the beacon technology market.

Moreover, government agencies around the world are focusing on developing smart city projects to modernize the urban infrastructure and create highly connected cities by leveraging cutting-edge technologies. Beacons are expected to play an important role in enabling such networks which can be managed at the micro-location level.

Beacon Technology Market, By Platform

The iBeacon platform is expected to dominate the market by 2024 with a significant market share of over 55% as the platform is the pioneer in introducing Bluetooth Low Energy (BLE) wireless technology. As various vendors aggressively began manufacturing and commercializing iBeacon compatible beacon transmitters soon after Apple launched this platform in 2013, it received the first mover's advantage and captured a major share of the beacon technology market.

The market share of Eddystone by Google, being the prime competitor of iBeacon, is expected to grow with the highest CAGR between 2017 and 2024, primarily because of the vast user-base using android mobile devices. As Google is constantly integrating its other widely popular services such as Google Maps with the platform, along with the Chrome support for Eddystone launched in 2016, the number of Eddystone compatible beacons is projected to increase exponentially over the timeline.

Beacon Technology Market, By Deployment Model

The on-premise deployment model holds the major share of the beacon technology market in 2016, and it is expected to maintain this dominance by 2024 as most of the beacon manufacturers offer low-cost beacon transmitters which makes it highly affordable even for small businesses to deploy them with minimal computing infrastructure.

But, with increasing adoption of cloud computing technology and its capability to effectively manage large fleets of beacons deployed across wider geographical areas, the cloud deployment model is expected to exhibit fastest growth during the forecast period.

Beacon Technology Market, By Application

The retail sector holds the most significant share of the market in 2016 and will maintain the largest market share by 2024 due to the large-scale adoption of beacon technology by retailers to efficiently implement proximity marketing campaigns. As it allows the retailers to push location-specific as well as customer-specific marketing messages onto the customers' mobile devices in real-time, the success rate of marketing campaigns can be significantly improved.

The healthcare sector is projected to witness high growth during the timeline owing to the capability of proximity beacons to enable improved healthcare management systems including efficient patient tracking, asset monitoring and healthcare security and compliance. With vendors introducing beacons designed specifically for use in sensitive hospital environments, the adoption is estimated to accelerate over the timeline.

Beacon Technology Market, By Technology

BLE dominates the beacon technology market in 2016 with a major market share of over 85% due to its low power consumption capabilities compared to other technologies in the market such as Wi-Fi, Geofencing and GPS. As it is cheaper to manufacture BLE modules, the overall cost of beacon hardware can be significantly reduced which makes the technology the most preferred choice for operating beacons.

The technology is expected to grow with the highest CAGR between 2017 and 2024 as more and more retailers are adopting BLE beacons to cost-effectively deploy and manage proximity marketing campaigns and increase customer revisits and impulse purchases. Due to their highly affordable nature, larger networks of BLE beacons can be implemented for a relatively low cost compared to other wireless technologies.

Beacon Technology Market, By Region

North America is projected to dominate the beacon technology market by 2024 owing to the extensive adoption of the technology in the region, especially in the retail sector. Large scale U.S. retailers such as Walmart and Target have deployed beacons in numerous retail stores for beaming promotions, coupons, store maps and product info via their mobile apps. As traditional retailers in the region are becoming more adept at using technology to sustain against e-commerce retail models, beacons have emerged as the go to technology to enable a rich digital shopping experience for their customers.

With increasing emphasis on improving the technology infrastructure and a booming retail sector, the APAC market is expected to grow steadily over the forecast period. With increasing awareness about beacon technology in countries such as Japan, Australia and India, the market will grow with the highest CAGR between 2017 and 2024.

Retail

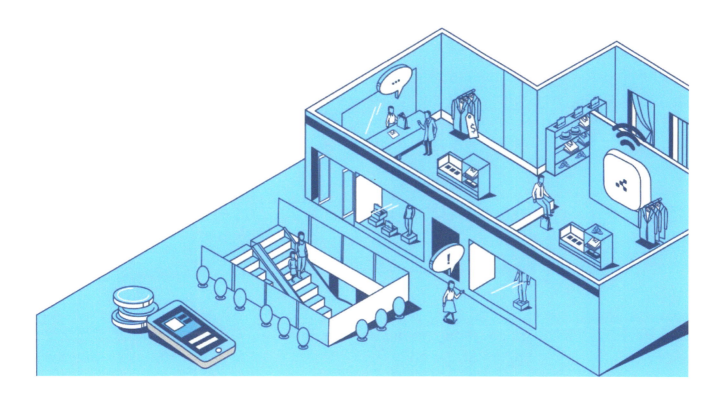

Retail is one of the most experienced and fast-growing industries using beacons today. In fact, Business Insider predicted that in 2016, beacons would directly influence over $40 billion worth of US retail sales at top 100 retailers.

There are four key use cases for beacons in retail. Best of all, with a proper infrastructure, you don't have to pick just one. Creative managers can use these as a starting point to generate more nuanced projects.

K-supermarket uses beacons for better in-store conversion rates

Popular Finnish chains K-supermarket and K-citymarket used digitized shopping carts to reach customers at the moment of decision. With the help of SmartCart, the chain is now delivering 250,000 smart ads per day and offering all new capabilities to their customers. More importantly, 84% of their users plan to use the SmartCarts on their next visit.

ELLE drives 21,000 in-store visits with beacons

ELLE partnered with ShopAdvisor to outfit 803 locations with beacons. They used beacons in retail to provide more contextual data and promotions to shoppers. Thanks to carefully crafted messaging, they brought 8.5% of their shoppers in store. That's 10,000% better than the average mobile advertising campaign. Overall, this has been one of the single most successful mobile advertising campaigns yet, and they've got the metrics to prove it. It's estimated the program generated up to $440K revenue for participating brands. Is this the future of shopping?

Carrefour gains 600% more app users by enabling proximity

$20B+ multinational retailer Carrefour used mobile apps for two years before realizing it was time for an upgrade. They enriched one with proximity, and now they can communicate with shoppers better than ever. Beacons deployed at the store welcome shoppers as they enter, display coupons, and suggest products based on the purchase history. After 7 months Carrefour observed that the number of app downloads increased by 600%, and users spend 400% more time in the app. Even for huge, immensely successful retailers, beacons add that something special.

Gino Rossi drives 99% retention rate in its loyalty program

Gino Rossi is a leading Polish manufacturer of luxurious footwear. They integrated a beacon-enabled app with their existing omni channel platform in order to provide users with super-targeted offers based on previous purchases and behavior. By delivering relevant content to the right audience, at the right place, and at the right time, Gino Rossi has been able to retain 99% of retention over time and achieve a click-through rate of 85%.

Ebizu takes over the Asian market with proximity

Ebizu is a robust platform for beacons in retail that helps drive sales, engage with customers, and analyze marketing efforts. It uses proximity to bring context to day-to-day activities and amplify customers' shopping experience. Beacons installed in malls notify users about sales and products based on previous shopping behavior and engagement history and enable a hands-free check-in, allowing visitors to them seamlessly collect loyalty points.

Vulcano Buono gamifies malls with beacons

Beacons the large Vulcano Buono shopping center in Italy provide app users with everything they need to shop smarter including coupons for boutiques they're passing, promotions for nearby restaurants, or even upcoming movies at a movie theater they're approaching. Here's where it gets fun: users earn points by interacting with beacon-triggered content in the dedicated app. High scores at the right time means awesome prizes.

This is a great example of how beacons in retail can do more than just send promos.

Rockbot personalized playlists, boosts check-ins 41%

Rockbot is a virtual jukebox that connects brands and customers through proximity and music. It provides stores, restaurants, and gyms with beacons, and customers with a beacon-enabled app that wakes up as a user enters a venue to add his or her favorite song to the ongoing playlist. This customer-focused approach resulted not only in hundreds of delighted customers, but also increased the number of check-ins per venue by 41% and boosted song request rates by 22%.

HotSpot turns 30% of its users into local stores' visitors

HotSpot is a Canadian parking solution that basically does two things: help drivers solve their parking problems and drive foot traffic into brick-and-mortar stores and restaurants. It enables users to easily top up parking time through a mobile app anywhere they are—thanks to that, they don't have to worry about getting parking tickets and can enjoy their hassle-free shopping. And in order to enhance the shopping experience even more, HotSpot notifies its users about interesting venues and promotions nearby and once they walk in, they can count on VIP service and perks, such as free parking top up. As a result, 30% of HotSpot users who park near a HotSpot-enabled location visit it and then stays there 13% longer than other visitors.

Volkswagen drives customers to explore

Auto Ganza, an official Volkswagen dealer in Moscow, deployed beacons at its showroom to help its visitors freely explore cars and their capabilities. When a prospect approaches a model, a dedicated beacon-enabled app, developed by iBecom, triggers information about its cost, technical specifications, and available colors. If someone finds this information exciting, he or she can schedule a test drive—right from the app.

T-Systems is also using beacons to reduce churn by providing better service to visitors.

Brixton Pound makes mobile payments easier

Brixton Pound is a cryptocurrency used by consumers in Brixton to pay for products and services. In 2011, Brixton Pound switched from paper currency to pay-per-text. Three years later, they facilitated the process even more by launching a beacon-enabled app developed by DingoLabs. Now, users don't have to text to pay; as they walk into Brixton Pound enabled venue, they simply tap a beacon-triggered notification on their smartphone screens and their payments are processed.

Sizeer boosts customer loyalty

Sizeer is a multi brand street fashion chain with 14+ stores in East-Central Europe countries. In order to increase engagement and retention of almost 500,000 customers using the brand's loyalty club, Sizeer implemented proximity into its strategy and launched a beacon-enabled loyalty app, SizeerClub. Beacons deployed at all Sizeer's stores notify users about ongoing promotions, trigger personalized offers, and serve information about products that a customer is looking at.

Franck Muller gives a beacon-enabled app to its sales representatives

Franck Muller is known for luxurious watches and VIP service. In order to make the customer experience even more extraordinary, the brand equipped its sales representatives with a beacon-enabled app for iPads, created by Pixeltrade. The app, integrated with Franck Muller's POS provides them with information about products, enables them to place orders including selecting dimensions and materials such as the dial color and all possible options. Everything through the app, and the representatives don't have to manually search products because the app displays those that are in the closest proximity.

Beacons in Retail Mean Big Data

Personalization improves email message click-through rates by an average of 14% and conversions by 10%. Customers expect personalization. How can companies make it happen? Think beacons in retail are just for looks? Here's how they're changing the way businesses do data.

Can beacons bring new opportunities with big data for retail? Numbers indicate we may see beacons in retail driving more data soon.

Retailers around the world are still learning how to work with data. Since the introduction of modern data analytics in the 1990s, the market has been preparing for technology to change the way we do business. Data analytics, of course, are not new. What is changing, however, are the possibilities of data analytics. The IoT means increased data generation, and retailers in particular are set to win big—or at least see big changes. Data means smarter campaigns, smarter resource management, and endless personalization for communications with customers.

Personalization with data is changing the way we shop. One study found[4]: "Personalized email messages improve click-through rates by an average of 14% and conversions by 10%."

What's holding retailers and proximity marketers back?

It's clear that big data in retail is no laughing matter. Unfortunately, it's not always easy to manage. Despite years of talk, many companies have yet to walk the walk, and there are several important reasons for this.

One reason retailers are not yet ready to play with big data is the cost and investment. How should retailers capture data? How should they efficiently plug data into their existing business? And how should they create a truly omnichannel marketing system? Despite the hype, excitement, and genuine possibilities, retailers must be prepared to answer all these **questions before moving forward.**

---

[4] https://www.campaignmonitor.com/blog/email-marketing/2016/01/70-email-marketing-stats-you-need-to-know/

Health Care

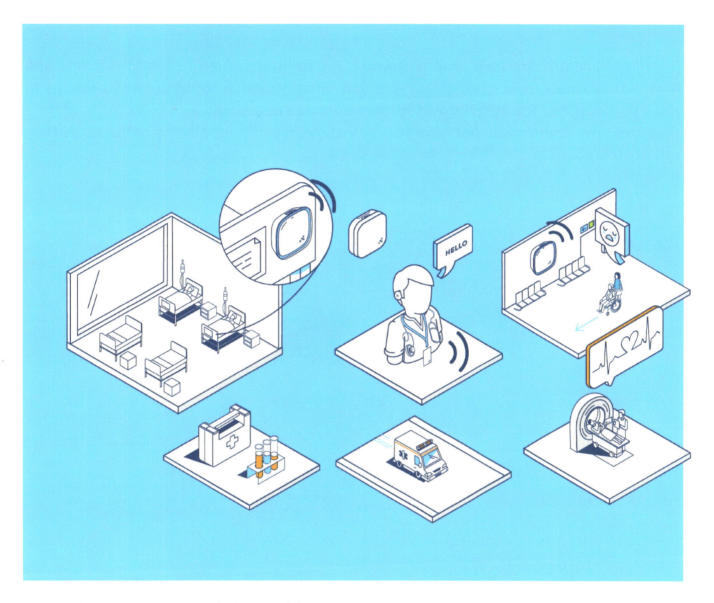

Hospital operators around the world are using IoT to give patients a better experience and reduce wasted funds and resources. With Bluetooth tags and beacons, healthcare companies can quickly increase asset utilization, ease wayfinding, optimize patient flow, and more without overpaying. In this section we'll discuss some case studies.

The University Hospital Basel provides wayfinding across 50 clinics

The largest healthcare facility in northwest Switzerland needed to provide visitors and staff with a smart indoor navigation solution. infsoft used 2,500 Bluetooth beacons to make that happen. The hospital was further surprised to learn about the long-life of their infrastructure, and they do not have to worry about regularly replacing batteries as they initially feared.

Supply Chain

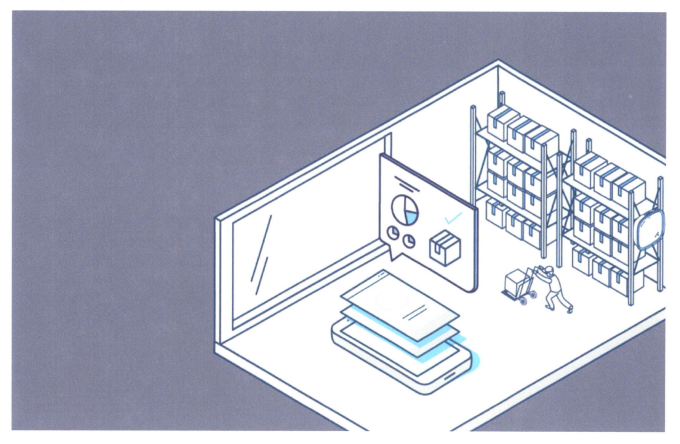

With Beacon-based warehouse solutions gaining traction, the near future of the supply chain looks highly digitized. The most popular use cases include forklift, pallet, and employee tracking, reducing search times, and temperature monitoring in cold chain logistics.

Zence tracks Skanska employees for safety with 93% accuracy

Skanska Construction needed a solution that would confirm the entry and exit of workers from the tunnel in accordance with Norwegian laws. Zence used 2 Gateways to cover the 300m space inside the tunnel. They equipped each worker with one Bluetooth beacon whose signal could be read even as the employee drove past. The cards were read at 80km/h with 93% accuracy, largely automating the process and reducing the number of times workers had to exit their vehicles.

Events

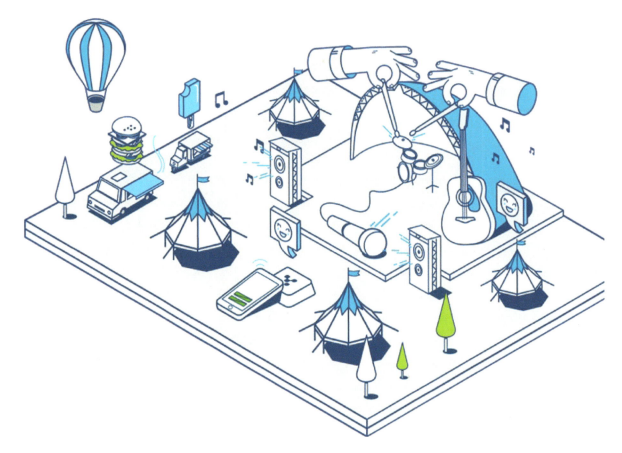

Proximity powers events around the globe—from local meetups to huge expos and conferences. Learn how event planners use beacons to connect with attendees and get more out of event apps.

Mobile World Congress boosts its app engagement 235%

People attending Mobile World Congress 2015 could enjoy a conference app enriched with proximity by MOCA. Beacons enabled seamless ticketing and mobile check-ins at main entrances, proximity-aware notifications about exhibitors, and information at transportation as users left the venue. As a result, 47% of mobile users interacted with the app at the venue.

ACE of M.I.C.E Exhibition makes business card exchange seamless

Pointr beaconized a whole conference venue to enable its visitors to seamlessly exchange business cards. Thanks to beacons, as a user approached an exhibitor's stand, he or she could exchange contact information with a representative by simply waving his or her smartphone. All the new contacts were saved in the app so attendees could access them during or after the event.

eFan24 engages 80% of users by making a stadium more interactive

PGE Arena in Gdansk launched a proximity-enabled eFan24 app to answer the needs of the new generation of sports fans. The app helps users move around the stadium, prompts them to share their emotions every time something important happens, and promotes hot deals and promotions. As a result, 83% of users click on beacon-triggered messages, and 80% out of them interact further with them.

The Bonnaroo Festival personalized the attendee experience

The Bonnaroo Festival used beacon-enabled FestApp by Aloompa to deliver personalized, proximity-aware notifications about events and facilities nearby to the attendees.

iCON Prague encourages attendees to network

iCON Prague, a series of events dedicated to creativity, life hacking, and smart technologies, deployed proximity at its venue to gamify the event experience. Beacons triggered invitations to visit the nearby exhibitors' stands, exchange contact information, and find key points in the venue. For interacting with proximity-based content, the visitors would get points that they could then exchange for event-related gadgets and souvenirs. As a result, 60% of app users performed at least 45 interactions.

TEDxPadova reduced printing costs 45%

TEDxPadova used beacons and a beacon-enabled app developed by AzzuroDigitale to provide attendees with information about nearby exhibitors, the venue, ongoing events, and other attractions. Since the app provided all information visitors needed, the organizers could reduce the amount of printed materials like signs and programs. As a result, they saved 45% on printing.

Expo Milano 2015 gave a mobile assistant to its attendees

Accenture leveraged proximity to give visitors a unique experience at the Universal Exhibition of Milan, making it an innovative digital event. Beacons provided attendees with mobile a map of a venue, seamless check-in system, events agenda, coupons, and customized journals of events.

Houston Dynamo rewards loyal fans

Houston Dynamo added beacons to their loyalty app to trigger reminders about ongoing contests and challenges to the users while they're watching games. For the club, it was a more contextual way to engage with its fans when they were on the spot and a way to connect fans to sponsors. For the fans—just another opportunity to collect loyalty points that they can use to get gadgets with their favorite color of orange.

Palexpo boosts the fair trade experience

Planet Intus SA beaconized Palexpo's huge trade show hall to empower visitors to find their location in exhibition halls, be guided to points of interest, and receive messages from exhibitors.

Panorama Berlin's indoor navigation engages 70% of users

Panorama Berlin is a huge fashion expo that wanted to make navigating the venue easier to visitors. They partnered up with LabWerk to add an indoor navigation feature to their existing app. The feature, showing a route to a selected booth, was used more than once by 70% of the app users.

Electric Castle Festival gamifies the music festival experience

In order to encourage attendees to promote the festival's attractions, the event planners partnered up with Zoniz Proximity to provide a treasure hunt. Attendees who downloaded the app were challenged to visit particular areas and solve puzzles to move to the next step. All of that for fun experience and great prizes.

The Reeperbahn Festival helps attendees remember events they saw

Reeperbahn Festival is a huge umbrella event consisting of 600 small events held in 70 different locations. In order to help attendees keep track of events they attended, the event planners launched Logbook, a feature built in an app developed by Greencopper. Thanks to beacons deployed on site, Logbook knows where an attendee was and, based on that, logs his or her activity in a personalized timeline of attended events.

Museums

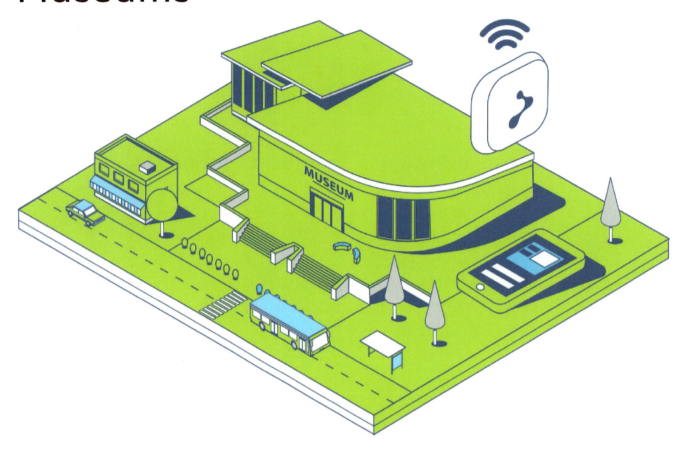

Proximity makes museums relevant in the XXI century by making them more interactive and changing the way they educate, guide, and tell stories. Find out how museums embrace proximity and use beacons to engage with visitors.

The de Young Museum takes visitor experience to the next level by combining beacons and Google Glass

The de Young Museum in San Francisco was looking for a technology that could augment—but not alter—the visitor experience during the Keith Haring's exhibition. They decided to go for Google Glass, but in order to make it more seamless, they integrated the Glass with beacons. Thanks to proximity, related content automatically shows up right before visitor's eyes once he or she approaches a piece of art.

Kew Gardens guides visitors around the site

One of the world's oldest botanic gardens, The Royal Botanic Gardens, Kew wanted to provide its visitors with proximity-aware educational content. The two technologies that they considered were beacons and WiFi, and they went for beacons. As a visitor with the Kew app installed walks in the range of a device, it triggers information, pictures, and videos about species nearby. Thanks to beacons, Kew Gardens was able to engage with their visitors in a new, interactive way and to save 90% over Wi-Fi.

Bristol Museum and Art Gallery provides indoor navigation

The Hidden Museum app presents visitors with physical journey around the museum—a journey full of paths, challenges, and mini games. All of these to encourage visitors to reveal elements of the museum they would not normally see, such as seldom visited galleries, collections not currently on display and behind-the-scenes stories, all of which can be taken home digitally and enjoyed away from the site.

Muzze replaces traditional audio guides for 3% of their price

40+ museums that use Muzze, a beacon-enabled app created with both curators and visitors in mind, don't have to worry about investing in and maintaining costly audio guide infrastructures. Muzze provides them with beacons and easy-to-use app that suggests recordings related to exhibits that a user is looking at. There's no need to rent and carry any extra equipment—visitors listen to the audio guide on their smartphones. This helps museums save 97% over traditional audio guides. What's more, their beacon-enabled tours are 240% more engaging!

The Philadelphia Museum of Arts connects families and pieces of art

Every summer, the Philadelphia Museum of Arts organizes Art Splash, a special program of events and activities dedicated to families. In 2015, the museum launched a beacon-enabled "A is for Art Museum" app to help visitors explore its exhibitions in an entertaining and child-friendly way. The app, installed on museum's iPads, challenges families to find 26 works of art throughout the Museum keyed to the letters of the alphabet. Beacons provide a way-finding tool and trigger content at these exhibits, such as additional information, audio, video, and real-world games to perform with the whole family.

MOCAK provides information about exhibits when you actually need it

MOCAK, the Museum of Contemporary Art in Krakow, Poland, deployed beacons next to selected exhibits to provide more information about artworks and their authors. When a visitor approaches a beaconized piece of art, an app developed by HG Intelligence triggers a notification with an incentive to learn more. After tapping on it, the user can read a detailed description, interview with an author, or other works by the artist.

The Eldheimar Museum generates 95% engagement by making audio guides seamless

The Eldheimar Museum in Iceland is dedicated to a volcano eruption in 1973 and consists of the remains of a buried village. The museum didn't want printed labels and signs to spoil this natural and dramatic landscape, so they decided not to use any. Instead, they used proximity and a dedicated app, developed by Locatify. The app provides an audio guide that, thanks to beacons, plays stories connected to areas where visitors are currently in. As a result, 95% of visitors listens to the whole tour.

Torino Zoom engages 60% of users by unlocking proximity-enabled content after a while

Torino Zoom is an immersion exhibit that educates visitors on wildlife. It uses beacons to make its tours more interactive but in order not to distract visitors, the app doesn't trigger proximity-enabled content immediately. Instead, it logs places that a user's seen and displays relevant content when he or she is in a leisure zone. This non-standard approach drives 60% engaged users and 25 interactions per user.

A Tough Beacon enables Cezar, the alpaca, to speak

Van Ons and Media 599 developed a proximity-enabled app and deployed beacons at Valleike farm to provide visitors with pictures, videos, games, and other edutainment experiences. One of the beacons is attached to an alpaca named Cezar, powering him to be even more cute and entertaining.

The City of Edinburgh guides its visitors through the Royal Mile on mobile without the Internet connection

The Edinburgh Up Close app, developed by Neatebox, takes city tours to the next level by making them personal, available to everyone (also to sight and hearing impaired users,) and possible to walk through at one's own pace. Beacons deployed along the Royal Mile trigger information and stories about streets, buildings, and museum that a user passes by. All the pieces of content may be read or listened to, accessed with or without an Internet connection, and consumed immediately or saved for later.

The National Portrait Gallery in London helps explore faces of Britain

The National Portrait Gallery used beacons and a beacon-enabled app developed by Locatify at the Face of Britain exhibition. Beacons located next to some key portraits automatically triggered relevant audio commentaries by Simon Schama, a historian, host of a BBC series, and author of a book entitled Face of Britain.

SeaWorld Orlando amuses conference attendees with beacon-enabled guide.

Attendees of The Garden Center Group's fall event in Orlando could not only enjoy the conference-related features, but also go for a VIP tour guide around the SeaWorld. Tough Beacons located at the park marked key places and help the users navigate the area. After reaching one of these points, a user had to interact with content in order to get directions on how to get to another.

The Palace of Venaria believes that context is king

The Palace of Venaria is a XVII-century royal residence that attracts visitors by its great story and beautiful architecture. To encourage the visitors to explore both, the palace staff rolled out the La Venaria app developed by Smart Beacon. Thanks to beacons installed on site, the app shows a map of available attractions that get unlocked only if a user visits them.

The Groninger Museum stimulates interactions between the museum, visitors, and exhibits

The Groninger Museum deployed beacons and use TapArt platform to engage visitors throughout their journey. Beacons trigger not only content about artworks in proximity, but also videos when visitors stay in line so they can start learning while waiting.

Sydney Art Project Uses Beacons to Share Aboriginal Culture

In partnership with Kaldor Public Art Projects, Australian artist Jonathan Jones[5], himself of Aboriginal origin, created an exhibition entitled "Barrangal Dyara" ("Skin and Bones"), to bring what was lost back to life for a new generation and to commemorate the priceless links with the past that were turned to ashes all those years ago.

---

[5] http://www.jonathanjones.com.au/

Omnichannel Marketing Gets Smarter with Beacons

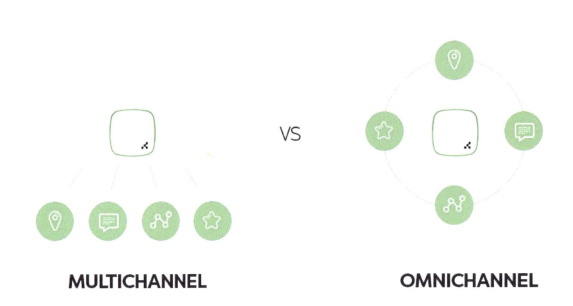

MULTICHANNEL   OMNICHANNEL

Omnichannel marketing is set to take over retail. So what's holding it back? Omni marketing needs smarter solutions if it wants to succeed.

The Omnichannel: perhaps the most epically named of all marketing topics. It does, however, completely deserve this title. It's very easy to assume omnichannel is just another fad, but for the near and distant future, it's going to play a pivotal role in how consumers engage with marketing campaigns.

Note that omni-marketing isn't just about how marketers would like to engage with customers. It's about how customers really behave and how marketers can offer the solutions they want.

What is Omnichannel and Multichannel retailing?

Omnichannel marketing is focused on creating a seamless customer experience, connecting all possible channels to make it easy for customers to move from one to the next and achieve greater success.

Most companies today work with a multichannel approach to customer interaction. Because customers want to use desktops, mobile devices, and even visit real brick and mortar stores, companies are forced to advertise and promote through each of these channels. You may get a special discount while surfing the web that you wouldn't receive in-store or vice versa.

Multichannel retailing can effectively enhance the customer experience, but there is one ingredient missing: integration.

All of these channels remain separated. What happens on one doesn't really affect the other. In other words, a customer may be creating a story on each individual channel, but there is no overarching story uniting them all. This means there's no one, complete image of the customer and their preferences. This is a huge missed opportunity for all parties. More importantly, it's a method that, in many ways, reflects the past. It reflects the introduction of new technologies and channels, but *not* the most efficient way to use them. One statistic makes this clear:

Over 90% of retail shoppers use their smartphone in store[6].

Whether it's a museum, a shopping mall, or a music festival, customers are all about mobile, all the time. They're about getting the most up-to-date and relevant information. But the standard for what is "relevant" is drastically changing. It's not enough to simply know that a user has signed up for a mailing list. It's not enough to know their gender or age. When your competitors are making offers that directly relate to an individual, you're going to have to add more, smarter fields to your customer profiles.

Here's where omnichannel marketing shines: it's all about creating the complete, unified story. The information logged in your desktop-browsing is paired with your in-store behavior and matched with your previous purchases. This is the proper omnichannel retail experience.

"You enter a store and aren't entirely sure what you're looking for. As you approach the seasonal section, you get a message: just a single, well-executed push notification. You've been eyeing a new pair of boots online for weeks and, now that you're in the store, you receive a discount. You also receive a full list of

---

[6] http://blog.sessionm.com/how-can-retailers-create-the-same-buzzworthy-experiences-as-amazon-go

matching items that fit with your previous purchases. When you have trouble, a customer service representative can quickly identify your needs and get you the answers you never knew you needed."

The numbers show omnichannel's strengths

One study[7] found that only 7% of shoppers shopped *only* online. 20% shopped *only* in-store. The remainder? The remaining 73% would use multiple channels. Importantly, these shoppers would also log more in-store visits, purchases, and likelihood of recommending the brand to others.

The catch with omnichannel marketing

A survey from Accenture and hybris software, an SAP company, found that nearly 40% of retailers are having difficulty integrating back-office technology across offline, online, and mobile. This should come as no surprise.

It's somewhat easy to create a multichannel retailing system. You add a department here or a campaign there. Omnichannel, however, requires unification. Everything must work together seamlessly. From the technology to the data and marketing pushes, everything must be planned with a unified objective. It will take time for companies to adequately prepare and master omnichannel marketing. How do you even go from one channel to the other? Perhaps more importantly, how do you go from digital to physical?

Company culture has to change. In order to implement a thoroughly omnichannel marketing approach, numerous departments (if not every last one) has to buy into the new system. Designers and programmers must understand how fluid and directed each channel must be. Marketers must appreciate that each section is as important as the rest. And all of the surrounding teams-and executives-need to respect the required effort in order to achieve proportionate returns. This also means always addressing any silos or bottlenecks. When communication between channels break down, the overall effect is immediately dampened.

---

[7] https://hbr.org/2017/01/a-study-of-46000-shoppers-shows-that-omnichannel-retailing-works

Getting started with omnichannel

Step 1. Push communication between departments

From IT to marketing, successful omnichannel efforts require an amount of fluidity. As users move from desktop to mobile to in-store or the company hotline, efforts must be completely unified and seamless. Each department must understand the customer, the pains and goals, and how everyone is working together to make that experience happen. Strive for consistency.

Step 2. Understand the customer better

Personalizing messages and keeping a customer on track doesn't happen by accident. Teams must step back and reexamine their users, how they move, and what their needs are. Where does your user need to be spoken to? When are they most receptive and why? It's possible to skip this step and use generalized messages. However, that would completely undermine the power of a fluid, omnichannel system. Outline what your users need and where you should deliver what information to create clear results.

Step 3. Consider context

Where is your user now? What pushes someone to buy at home in their PJs isn't likely to work when they're on their way to work in the morning. While this method of communication can be more complicated for marketers, it also supplies more opportunities for high converting messages and actions. By targeting the user's needs based on their actual context and location, businesses can achieve far higher results and also keep customers happier by providing useful, actionable opportunities.

Beacon-based omnichannel marketing

"The real opportunity is mobile leading retail," **says**[8] Rob Murphy, vice president of marketing for mobile presence platform Swirl Networks. "It's a great connection between the physical and the digital. Most people have a mobile device in their hands. With the technology available in the phone, you know when the consumer is in the store, what items they might like (in-store or online)."

If you think mobile is important now, give it a few more years. Generation Z will elevate the importance of mobile technology to a completely new (hopefully omnichannel) level.

---

[8] http://www.enterpriseappstoday.com/crm/omni-channel-retailers-try-beacons.html

The role of mobile, however, is not just to give customers a chance to browse digitally from any location. It's also not just for sending digital messages. It's the power of **proximity**.

After proper back-end integration and planning, proximity to specific products, goods, or services is the key to creating the seamless flow from online to offline. This will be done primarily through technology like Bluetooth beacons.

What are beacons? (read section What is a Beacon)

You've heard about them for years. You've even heard about their uses in marketing, but it has taken time for businesses to understand how to properly use them. Businesses are beginning to understand that beacons are **useless when leveraged improperly**. This has been blocking the shift from multi to omnichannel marketing for some time, now. However, more use cases emerging in success, sometimes huge, inspiring success-personal favorite comes from **ELLE**. It's clear beacons are on the path to becoming ubiquitous with omni marketing.

How do beacons build up omnichannel marketing?

Beacons are those small Bluetooth-based devices that can communicate with your smartphone. Most importantly, they may say different things depending on where you stand in the physical world. If you're in a cafe, they may offer you a discount on a slice of cake. If you're maneuvering a festival, they can offer up-to-date information about shows or even recommend events based on your history. If you visit your favorite store, they can ping you with information about your loyalty points, what you've earned, and even replace the physical card itself—so you don't have to worry about ever losing it, or overstuffing your wallet, again!

On top of simply creating a channel to perfectly and effectively address your customers at the moment of choice, beacons can combine with omni marketing campaigns to:

- Make loyalty programs more efficient
- Collect and utilize relevant data
- Enable faster or automated transactions
- Power better and easier couponing practices

Beacons in Retail Bring New Data Opportunities

We discussed the area briefly in the Retail section, here we'll explore in more detail the role of beacons and data in the retail space. So can beacons bring new opportunities with big data for retail? Numbers indicate we may see beacons in retail driving more data soon.

Retailers around the world are still learning how to work with data. Since the introduction of modern data analytics in the 1990s, the market has been preparing for technology to change the way we do business. Data analytics, of course, are not new. What is changing, however, are the possibilities of data analytics. The IoT means increased data generation, and retailers in particular are set to win big—or at least see big changes. Data means smarter campaigns, smarter resource management, and endless personalization for communications with customers.

Personalization with data is changing the way we shop. One study found[9]: "Personalized email messages improve click-through rates by an average of 14% and conversions by 10%."

---

9 https://www.campaignmonitor.com/blog/email-marketing/2016/01/70-email-marketing-stats-you-need-to-know/

What's holding retailers and proximity marketers back?

It's clear that big data in retail is no laughing matter. Unfortunately, it's not always easy to manage. Despite years of talk, many companies have yet to walk the walk, and there are several important reasons for this.

One reason retailers are not yet ready to play with big data is the cost and investment. How should retailers capture data? How should they efficiently plug data into their existing business? And how should they create a truly omnichannel marketing system? Despite the hype, excitement, and genuine possibilities, retailers must be prepared to answer all these questions before moving forward.

How can you use data from beacons in retail?

✓ Track footfall
✓ Create heatmaps
✓ Analyze merchandising effectiveness
✓ Gauge customer loyalty
✓ Enable personalized communications
✓ Optimize scheduling and resources

How beacons in retail work

Bluetooth beacons are an incredibly hot buzz word these days. Big data, IoT, beacons—retailers want all of it. However, many retailers don't quite understand how beacons even work. The beacon hardware is exceedingly simple. It broadcasts a single message at regular intervals that is then picked up by Bluetooth-enabled devices. This message is nothing special. In fact, it's more or less just the ID number, indicating which beacon it is. The real magic happens elsewhere.

Key terms for using data and beacons in retail:

Advertising Identifier (IDFA) is a unique ID for iOS devices

Advertising ID is an ID provided by Google Play services

Both of these identifiers achieve the same results—tracking users from the digital and physical worlds. Think of them like a cutting-edge cookie. They track actions not only online but across devices and even in apps. Luckily for solution providers, there's not much difference between the two fundamentally. Most importantly, these consistent IDs make it much easier for businesses or developers to interact and understand data.

Then, there's **Attribution**. Attribution is about understanding exactly who is receiving a message. Instead of just throwing a message out into the wild, or knowing only that it went to faceless, nameless, altogether information-less user is a very way short-term thinking. Attribution tells the app or program manager who is receiving what messages and whether they're interacting with messages. Attributing interaction (or lack thereof) to specific users in specific spaces creates the kind of data that can prove whether an ad is working. Now, you can begin to see exactly what makes a message successful and what can be improved.

Solution providers design apps and platforms that make this location information valuable. With the beacon's identification information, an app can recognize that the user is located in the make-up section or at the exit. Again, very basic data. It's combining all these little points into Big Data that creates insights.

Knowing that your customer entered, received and engaged with a personalized promotion on mobile is a pretty interesting data point. So what happens next? Did your users go straight for the promoted product? Did they completely ignore it? Did many similarly grouped users buy the same product? All these little data points add up to insight for retailers. But it's up to solution providers to find out what data is valuable and how to capture, store, and display it. It's up to these innovative companies and start-ups to turn data into the footfall metrics and heatmaps described above.

This proximity data is what makes beacons irreplaceable. Other methods of data tracking simply cannot compile location data in the same way. Thomas Walle, CEO of proximity data platform Unacast, explains to Marketing Land[10]:

"The data is 100 percent deterministic and we can understand what people have been doing inside stores, in specific departments and interacted with different products. This granularity does [not exist] at Facebook, Google or any other company."

Real beacons in retail case study:

How one startup found food was key to driving returns

Startup Favendo installed beacons in the popular Les Terrasses du Port shopping center in Marseille. With 190 shops, the mall had plenty of untapped data for the beacons to illuminate.

For customers, the app used push notifications to make shopping more enjoyable. For business in the mall, the app meant insight into how customers moved both in individual retailers and around the space in general. Uptake has been key to driving results. Downloaded over 69,650 times and boasting an average 18 minute view time, the app effectively captured data points on how users moved.

72% of shoppers who stopped to eat kept shopping

Through data analysis, managers saw that too many shoppers were exiting the mall after visiting a handful of anchor stores. Other shoppers, however, would stop for a snack. Of these who stopped, 72% would continue shopping.

Looking closer, they found food options in the mall were often packed at peak times, driving away would-be diners and shoppers. Their response? Make more space in the food court. This increased dwell times of all customers who visited the anchor store by 42%.

Beacons in Retail mean personalization

Personalized promotions are the bread-and-butter of beacon popularity. Customers expect personalization, and an increasing number of studies are finding that users are willing to swap data for better experiences. One study from Salesforce[11] surveyed over 7,000 customers and had absolute unbelievable findings.

"If customers don't receive the level of customization they expect, they won't hesitate to shop around. More than half (52%) of consumers are somewhat likely

---

[10] http://marketingland.com/proximity-beacon-data-now-making-way-dsps-retargeting-198351
[11] https://www.salesforce.com/blog/2016/11/swap-data-for-personalized-marketing.html

to switch brands if a company doesn't make an effort to personalize their communications to them."

That's it. Customers simply won't stick around if they don't feel brands and retailers are living up to their expectations. More importantly, with all the options and successful personalized campaigns out there, these shoppers will find what they're looking for.

Beacons enable the connection of offline and online data as well as the chance to streamline omnichannel marketing tactics.

A study from Experian[12] found that personalized promotion messages received a 29% higher open rate and 41% higher click rate.

How beacons drive personalization in proximity marketing

It's all about the app. Again, solution providers are key when it comes to providing value with beacon data in retail. It's the platform that will connect a user's past purchases and online shopping persona with their real-world location.

Segmenting is key. 35-40 years old female shoppers who saved the same item in their online basket are drastically different from other segments, and they should receive messages that reflect their needs. If social authentication is required, that's yet another key ingredient to personalized communications.

Data on these repeat customers is also the most valuable for retailers. A major study from BIA/Kelsey and Manta[13] found that, of companies surveyed, 61% earned more than half their revenue from repeat customers. These repeat customers spend 67% more than new customers.

What does this mean for retailers?

Retailers are installing hundreds of thousands of beacons. A recent Proxbook Report found that data monetization and proximity retargeting are continuing as the fastest growing proximity services. IBM[14] found that **62% of retailers report analytics and data as a competitive advantage for their company.** Industry guru Stephen Statler estimated[15] expected US retailers to purchase over a million beacons in 2016 for deployment. The only real question is how solution providers will fit into the scene. Beacon data and capabilities are increasingly coveted by retailers and managers, so how can solution providers craft apps to get the most of data? Which companies and platforms will be successful and how will they surprise us?

---

[12] https://www.experianplc.com/media/news/2014/experian-marketing-services-study-finds-personalized-emails-generate-six/

[13] http://blog.biakelsey.com/index.php/2014/04/03/biakelsey-and-manta-joint-report-smbs-shift-priority-to-customer-retention/

[14] https://www-935.ibm.com/services/us/gbs/thoughtleadership/big-data-retail/

[15] https://unacast.s3.amazonaws.com/Proximity_Marketing_in_Retail_-_Proxbook_Report.pdf

How retailers can use data from beacons in retail

Data analytics have been a major start-up topic for some years now. After many quarters in the spotlight, there are two key points most businesses can agree: first, big data, when properly leveraged, can be indispensable; second, big data can easily be misused.

It's easy to misunderstand the role of data. Given the title "big data," many instantly think the more data, the better. But this isn't the case. It's crucial that any businesses looking to use beacons in retail for data purposes first define what makes data valuable.

Does your data:

- describe the customer
- illuminate the customer journey
- support long-term analytics
- come with all the necessary tags
- have a planned usage

What's the real goal of your data?

Collecting data that just fills up silos (whether because it's not important or not usable) is a waste of time and resources. There are three key ways to reuse beacon data in a retail setting: in-store optimization, retargeting, and monetization. Each of these is very different and may require different kinds of data. For example, to optimize store layout, you may need to understand how customers move. To retarget users, you'll need to know a little about their history. To monetize, you'll have to be ready to work with other brands. Many of these companies who deal in monetization will have specific requirements.

Driving users

Beacons are in an unusual position. Many managers are left wondering: are consumers ready for them? Oftentimes, store visitors don't see value in beacon technology, and that isn't their fault. There are hugely successful and less-than-successful beacon campaigns in retail, and this is a problem businesses must address before moving forward. Marcin Kasz explained this perfectly for Proximity.Directory:

"Bluetooth beacons are not a cure-all. They are also not a superfluous channel to push tired marketing efforts. However, the blocker with beacons in retail is very seldom the technology; the problem is almost always the business model." - Marcin Kasz.

If businesses want to use beacons in retail to engage customers, they must begin by solving a problem. As the shoppers at Les Terrasses du Port demonstrated, there is always a way retailers can better themselves. As popular as the shopping destination was, visitors had needs that were going unmet, and they tuned in to beacons because they were useful. Companies are achieving incredible success with beacons because they put the user first and offered solutions their users would actually use. Many retailing apps are simply out of date and not fit for modern user expectations. It's not up to users to find value in apps and then download them. Retailers must show users that the apps are worthwhile.

Retailers using beacons in 2017, 2018, and beyond

When beacons first appeared on the retail scene several years ago, there was an explosion of interest. There were huge success stories splashed across magazine covers and incredible stories of high-tech interactions with shoppers. Many of the possible use cases for beacons in retail have already been tested. Almost everything has been done, and retailers now have magnitude of options to pull from. This year, stores are realizing that the real value of Bluetooth in their shops and storefronts is the possibility of long-term returns.

Data is emerging as a new, primary driver of value in the retail industry. Walle, when interviewed for our white paper on beacon data, put it this way:

"With beacons, there is an overfocus on in-store experience. With notifications, you get one magical moment and that's it. But the real value is when [businesses] understand it's a data capturing tool."

There's no doubt that users will continue to find value in push notifications, indoor navigation, and other use cases in their local stores. However, it's time for managers to begin thinking long-term and take hold of the data they generate every day. - **In short: as you plan to deploy evolving technologies like proximity beacons, it is good to know your beacon strategy, and know your data strategy.**

Beacons Infrastructure Management & Cost

The Bluetooth beacon market is growing as new applications are developing and existing solutions roll out at scale. With nearly one million devices managed in backend systems, the beacon manufacturing industry test and prototype, deploy, roll-out, and expand infrastructures to support additional use cases.

A good **Infrastructure Management** helps address the problems users face at each step of the beacon journey and bring affordable scalability to beacon proximity networks.

Because of scaling and security requirements, a cost is associated with the growth of a beacon network, the price can range from low to average, (on average between $1 and $3 per beacon per month, other associated fees are not mentioned here. Costs are network and project related.)

Getting started or "provisioning"

The Basics

For the most part beacons are plug-n-play, the first task is to set up the hardware and start building or integrating them into a solution. In less than one minute, the beacons can be configured with the right protocol, transmission distance, and interval.

Using a Management App, Gateway, the changes are applied from the backend and the hardware is ready to go.

Maintaining an infrastructure and keeping it future proof

The use case is in place, the application is running, and the beacons are deployed. As with all IoT projects, the solution is only as strong as each link of the chain.

Broadly, we need to ensure three things:

- We need to recognize problems with our devices when or - even better - before they occur.
- We must make maintenance cost-effective.
- We must ensure that the infrastructure is future proof.

An **Infrastructure Management solution** helps do this with flexibility and efficiency. Beacons can be organized by tags and venue, bulk manage all configurations and export the data reliably in a CSV or access it at any time through APIs.

Alerts can be designed when anomalies occur in the beacon infrastructure. Anomalies such as low battery level or potentially lost beacons that haven't been detected in a while. To make this cost-effective, all beacons' configurations are held in a backend designed for security at scale and flexibility. Integrating, the "end user", mobile devices with the beacon network, the customers help maintain an up-to-date picture of the network devices as the data is fed back to the backend.

Infographic: Smart Home Solution

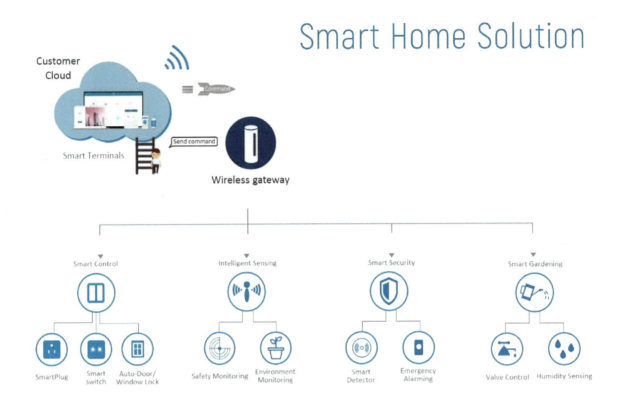

Smart Home Solution

Customer Cloud

Command

Send command

Smart Terminals

Wireless gateway

Smart Control
- SmartPlug
- Smart switch
- Auto-Door/ Window Lock

Intelligent Sensing
- Safety Monitoring
- Environment Monitoring

Smart Security
- Smart Detector
- Emergency Alarming

Smart Gardening
- Valve Control
- Humidity Sensing

www.ingramcontent.com/pod-product-compliance
Lightning Source LLC
Chambersburg PA
CBHW041431050326
40690CB00002B/507